Of Fatima

"Amen I say to you, whosoever shall not receive the kingdom of God as a little child, shall not enter into it." —Mark 10:15

OTHER BOOKLETS BY THE SAME AUTHOR

The Rosary and the Crisis of Faith

The Forgotten Secret of Fatima

St. Joseph, Fatima and Fatherhood

Fatima's Message for Our Times

I Wait For You (Editor)

Blessed Jacinta Marto Of Fatima

by

Msgr. Joseph A. Cirrincione

"Suffer the little children to come to me, and forbid them not; for of such is the kingdom of God." —Mark 10:14

TAN BOOKS AND PUBLISHERS, INC.
Rockford, Illinois 61105

This booklet was originally published (in 1992) as *Ven. Jacinta Marto of Fatima*.

ISBN 0-89555-782-7

Printed and bound in the United States of America.

TAN BOOKS AND PUBLISHERS, INC.
P.O. Box 424
Rockford, Illinois 61105

2005

"At that hour the disciples came to Jesus, saying: Who thinkest thou is the greater in the kingdom of heaven? And Jesus calling unto him a little child, set him in the midst of them, and said: Amen I say to you, unless you be converted, and become as little children, you shall not enter into the kingdom of heaven. Whosoever therefore shall humble himself as this little child, he is the greater in the kingdom of heaven."

—*Matthew 18:1-4*

CONTENTS

INTRODUCTION

I have written this booklet for two reasons: The first is in thanksgiving to the Immaculate Heart of Mary, who through the intercession of Jacinta and Francisco Marto, vouchsafed to restore me to health in 1990 when I was at death's door.

For many years, I had been praying for the beatification of Jacinta and Francisco Marto, having been spurred on by a quarterly newsletter from Father Luis Kondor, S.V.D., Vice Postulator for the Cause of their beatification.

Thus, when on July 8, 1990 I awakened during the night, suffering from chest pains that presaged a heart attack, I commended myself to their intercession. Taken to St. Mary's Hospital in Rochester, New York, I had to spend a week in the coronary intensive care unit. The doctors sought to correct the problem with medication. But, after a week, they informed me that open heart surgery was the only solution, which, they advised, was quite risky at my age—then 80 years old.

Since that type of operation is not performed at St. Mary's, I was transferred by ambulance to the Rochester General Hospital. Upon arrival, an angiogram was performed which revealed that an artery was 95% occluded. The doctors decided upon immediate surgery. Again, as I was prepared for the operation, I commended myself to the Immaculate Heart of Mary and to Jacinta and Francisco Marto.

I survived the operation, but two days later I suffered a cardiac arrest that damaged my heart and has since left me short of breath when I speak. Nonetheless, I was discharged from the hospital within a few days and was sent home.

However, within a week, I suffered a stroke and had to return to St. Mary's Hospital. Quite miraculously, it is my opinion, I suffered no permanent effects from the stroke—no paralysis and no brain damage. My prayers had been answered.

And this brings me to the second reason for writing this booklet; I want to encourage readers to join me in praying for the beatification of these two holy children, who were among the three visionaries at Fatima. (See Publisher's Note on p. 3.)

For I have another special grace for which to be thankful: On February 15, 1991, during a routine checkup by my doctor, an X-Ray of my chest was taken, which revealed a lesion in my lungs. Further surgery so soon after my heart surgery was likely to be fatal. So again, I turned to Jacinta and Francisco and prayed for their intercession on my behalf. The doctor offered me two options, surgery or prayer. I chose prayer.

On April 18, 1991, another X-Ray of my lungs was

taken. And wonderful to relate, the lesion was completely gone!

Therefore, in July of 1991, I went on a pilgrimage of thanksgiving to Fatima, taking with me the X-Rays of my lungs—before and after the lesion disappeared—along with a letter from the radiologist, explaining that there were no signs of the lesion or disease in my lungs.

In presenting the documentation to Father Kondor, I was told that April 18 was two years to the day since Jacinta and Francisco had been declared Venerable, though the public announcement was not made until the following May 13.

On April 15, 1992, another chest X-Ray of my lungs was taken; it still showed no signs of a nodule of any sort in my lungs. Providentially, friends of mine were going to Fatima in May, 1992, and they graciously consented to take the latest documentation to Father Kondor, together with the new X-Ray.

Msgr. Joseph A. Cirrincione
June 29, 1992
Feast of Sts. Peter and Paul

PUBLISHER'S NOTE

Jacinta and Francisco were beatified—declared Blessed—by Pope John Paul II in 2000.

Part I

THE THREE CHILDREN OF FATIMA

I first learned of the happenings at Fatima in 1947, when someone gave me a copy of a paperback edition of a book written by Finbar Ryan, then the Dominican Archbishop of Port-au-Prince, Haiti. It made a tremendous impression on me, and it amazed me that such extraordinary events could have occurred in 1917 *and* I was just then hearing of them, thirty years later. World War II had ended only two years before, and now I was reading that Our Lady had predicted it to three little children at Fatima, Portugal in 1917. This was something that I felt should be shouted from the housetops. I looked for other books on the subject and came across and read *The Crusade of Fatima* by Father John De Marchi, I.M.C. Next I obtained and read a copy of William Thomas Walsh's *Our Lady of Fatima,* as well as a book written by Barthas-Fonseca, entitled *Our Lady of Light.*

Equipped with this source material, I looked for an opportunity to share *The Story of Fatima* with a larger audience. The opportunity came when I discussed with a parishioner, who was program director of a local radio station, the possibility of doing just that by being given free air time. I succeeded in being given a half-hour every Sunday evening at 6:30 to tell *The Story of Fatima,* using the source material I had then compiled on Fatima. I began the series of talks on Sunday, January 11, 1948.

This is the story I told. There was in Portugal a small village or hamlet called Aljustrel. It was situated among the hills of a mountain range known as the Serra da Aire.

Here lived the three main characters of our story: Lucia dos Santos, who was born on March 22, 1907, the youngest of seven children of Antonio dos Santos and his wife, Maria Rosa; and Francisco and Jacinta Marto, Lucia's first cousins and the children of Manuel and Olimpia Marto. Olimpia was the sister of Lucia's father. Francisco was born June 11, 1908, and Jacinta on March 11, 1910. The two families were very close and lived on either side of a lane, for there were no streets as such in Aljustrel. Lucia's father owned a few parcels of land a short distance away that were used to graze the few sheep they owned and to grow vegetables for their table.

When the story of Fatima begins, Lucia's daily chore was each day to take the sheep out to graze. So strong was the attachment of Jacinta to her cousin, however, that she begged her mother to be able to go along with her, and therefore she was given a few sheep of her own to tend so that she and her brother could accompany their cousin to the hills.

Thus, the daily routine for the children was to

get up early each morning, and after a breakfast of bread and soup, and packing a small lunch for midday, the three would release their sheep from the pens and lead them out to the pastureland nearby.

One of Lucia's earlier companions recalled that "Lucia was a lot of fun, and we loved to be with her because she was always so pleasant. We did whatever she told us to do. She could sing and dance very well, and we could spend our whole day singing and dancing."

One day, probably in 1915, before her cousins began to join her, Lucia was accompanied by three other girls. As they recited the Rosary after lunch, all noticed the sudden appearance of a cloud in a form like that of a man, hovering above the foliage of the valley. Lucia describes what she saw as "like a cloud whiter than snow, slightly transparent, with a human outline." The impression this made on them remained for a while, but eventually it was forgotten.

About a year later, Lucia and her cousins, now her regular companions, went to a section of her father's land that lies at the foot of what is known as the Cabeco. About midmorning, it began to drizzle, and the children, seeking shelter, climbed the slope and entered a protected area. After the rain stopped and the sun had come out, and after their lunch and Rosary, they started to play "jacks."

Lucia recalls: "We played only a short while, when a strong wind shook the trees and made us raise our eyes to see what was happening, for the day was serene. There above the trees, toward the East, we began to see a light, whiter than snow. It was in the form of a young man, transparent, more brilliant than is crystal when pierced by the rays of the sun. We were so surprised, we could not utter one word. He came near us and said: 'Fear not! I am the Angel of Peace. Pray with me.' "

The Angel knelt on the ground and bowed very low. By some inspiration, the children imitated him and repeated the words they heard him pronounce: "My God, I believe, I adore, I hope and I love You. I beg pardon for those who do not believe, do not hope and do not love You." He repeated this prayer three times. Then he arose and said: "Pray this way. The Hearts of Jesus and Mary are attentive to the voice of your supplications."

After the Angel disappeared, they remained for some time in the same position in which he had left them, repeating the same prayer over and over again.

The prayerful mood that the children were in eventually dissipated, and they were soon back to their daily routine of playing, singing and dancing.

As the summer heat became more intense, the three sought the shade of the fig, almond and olive trees at noontime, near a well in Lucia's yard.

Suddenly, one day, the Angel appeared a second time, saying: "What are you doing? Pray! Pray a good deal. The Hearts of Jesus and Mary have designs of mercy for you. Offer unceasingly to the

Most High prayers and sacrifices!"

"But how are we to sacrifice ourselves?" Lucia said.

"Offer up everything in your power as a sacrifice to the Lord, as an act of reparation for the sins by which He is offended and of supplication for the conversion of sinners. Thus invoke peace upon our country. I am her Guardian Angel, the Angel of Portugal. Above all, accept and bear with submission the sufferings the Lord may send you."

Only Lucia and Jacinta heard the Angel's words. Francisco saw the Angel and knew he was speaking to the girls. Bursting with curiosity, he wanted to know what the Angel had said. "I will tell you tomorrow," Jacinta replied. "I am not able to speak to you now."

The next day, as soon as they got up, Francisco asked Jacinta, "Could you sleep last night? I was thinking of the Angel all night long, trying to guess what he said to you."

Lucia told him all the Angel had said. Jacinta added: "Take care, we must not speak of these matters."

In later years, Lucia revealed: "The words of the Angel were like a light that made us realize who God was, and He loved us and wanted to be loved; the value of sacrifice and to what degree it pleased Him, and how it was rewarded with the conversion of sinners. From that moment, we began to offer to the Lord everything that mortified us, without trying to find any other ways of mortification or penance." Later, "they passed hour after hour, bowed to the ground," repeating the prayer the Angel had taught them.

Along in late September, while the children were again tending their sheep, he appeared once more, beautiful, resplendent, dazzling, hovering in the air before them. This time, he held in one hand a chalice and in the other, over it, a Host. Leaving these suspended in the air, he prostrated himself on the ground and said: "Most Holy Trinity, Father, Son, Holy Spirit, I adore Thee profoundly and offer Thee the most precious Body, Blood, Soul and Divinity of Jesus Christ, present in all the tabernacles of the earth, in reparation for the outrages, sacrileges and indifference with which He Himself is offended. And through the infinite merits of His most Sacred Heart and of the Immaculate Heart of Mary, I beg of Thee the conversion of poor sinners."

He spoke these words three times. Then, rising up, he took the chalice and the Host, and kneeling on the flat rock, held them before him, saying:

"Take and drink the Body and Blood of Jesus Christ, horribly insulted by ungrateful men. Make reparation for their crimes and console your God."

They could see drops of Blood falling from the Host into the chalice. He placed the Host on Lucia's tongue. To Jacinta and Francisco, he presented the chalice, and they drank of it. Then, he prostrated himself once more on the ground and said the same prayer three times. The children repeated it with him. And then he was gone. As previously, Francisco had not heard the Angel speak, and he was anxious to learn everything.

"Lucia," he said, "I know that the Angel gave

you Holy Communion. But what did he give me and Jacinta?"

"The same," Jacinta replied with joy. "Did you not see it was the Blood that dropped from the Host?"

"I felt that God was within me," he agreed, "but I did not know how."

The three remained kneeling on the ground for a long time, repeating over and over again the prayer of the Angel.

The month of May saw nature on the Serra revive after its long winter sleep. Spring flowers appeared like jewels to adorn the earth.

On Sunday, May 13, while World War I was raging like a fire over Europe, Lucia and her little companions met as usual after Mass, accompanied by the sheep, which, this day, they led to a deep hollow known as the Cova da Iria.

Leaving their sheep to graze about, when they heard the church bells ring in the distance, knowing it was time for the last Mass, they said the Rosary and chased up the hill to play.

It was a bright, cloudless day, and when they saw what seemed like a flash of lightning they became frightened and started down the hill. They were passing a tall oak tree when another shaft of light split the air. They stopped, turned to the right and there, standing over the foliage of the holmoak, they saw a beautiful Lady, all dressed in white. "Fear not," the Lady said. "I shall do you no harm."

Lucia summoned courage enough to ask:

"Where do you come from?"

"I come from Heaven."

"From Heaven! And why have you come here?"

"I have come to ask you to come here for six months in succession on the thirteenth of each month, at this same hour. In the month of October, I shall tell you who I am and what I want."

"Could you tell me if the war will end soon?"

"I cannot tell you that until I have told you what I want."

"You come from Heaven! What about me—shall I go to Heaven?"

"Yes, you will go to Heaven."

"And Jacinta?"

"Jacinta also."

"And Francisco?"

The Lady turned toward the little fellow and looked at him with an expression of kindness and motherly reproach.

"He will go also, but he must first recite many Rosaries."

"Is little Maria das Neves who died recently in Heaven?"

"Yes, she is in Heaven."

"And Amelia?"

"She will be in Purgatory till the End of the World."

Then the Lady asked a favor.

"Would you like to offer yourselves to God, to make sacrifices and to accept willingly all the sufferings it may please Him to send you, in order to make reparation for so many sins which offend the Divine Majesty, to obtain the conversion of sinners, and to make amends for all the blasphemies and offenses committed against the Immaculate Heart of Mary?"

"Yes, we should like that very much."

"You will soon have much to suffer, but the grace of God will help you and give you the strength you need."

At these words, the Lady opened her hands. There emanated from them a beam of light so intense and deep that, penetrating their breasts even to the inmost depths of their souls, it made them see themselves in God, more clearly than in the clearest mirror.

Then, in Lucia's words, "moved by an irresistible force, we threw ourselves on our knees repeating fervently: 'O Most Holy Trinity, I adore You. My God, I love You.'"

Some moments later the Lady recommended them to recite the Rosary devoutly every day, to obtain peace for the world.

And then, gliding through space without moving her feet, the Lady departed towards the East, and disappeared in the light of the sun.

Gradually, the children returned to themselves, and, looking for the sheep, they found them grazing nearby. They spent the rest of the afternoon in the fields, living over and over again the short visit of Our Lady. Meanwhile, Francisco pressed the girls with questions to learn what she had said. (Francisco was not privileged to hear Our Lady's voice.) They told him everything. When they told him Our Lady promised that he would go to Heaven, but must say many Rosaries, he folded his hands in front of his breast and exclaimed: "O my Lady, I will say all the Rosaries you want." Lucia thought it best to keep the vision secret. Francisco and Jacinta agreed to do so. Lucia, however, had her doubts about Jacinta's ability to keep it secret, warning her: "I just know you are going to tell everyone."

"Honest, I will not tell anyone," she assured her. But she just could not keep her promise. Her parents had been away for the day, and when they returned, Jacinta, thinking of the beautiful Lady and forgetting her promise, rushed to tell her mother: "I saw Our Lady in the Cova da Iria." Olimpia's reaction was one that could be expected. "You silly girl, as if Our Lady would appear to a little girl like you!"

Ti Marto, as he was called, was finishing his chores in the barn, and then came in for supper. It happened that Antonio, Lucia's father, was there. During the meal, Olimpia mentioned what Jacinta had told her. The child needed no urging, and speaking with great excitement she repeated all she had told her mother. Lucia's father quietly took it all in, but said nothing to his wife when he returned home. But the next day, the story began to spread among the neighbors. It finally reached Lucia's eldest sister, Maria dos Anjos, who questioned Lucia whether the story were true.

"Jacinta couldn't keep a secret," she said. When questioned further she admitted they had seen a beautiful Lady.

"And what did she tell you?"

"She wanted us to go to the Cova for six months

and then she would tell us who she is and what she wants."

At this point, Francisco came along and confirmed Lucia's suspicion that it was Jacinta who had blurted out the whole story. Lucia's mother, who was much stricter with her children than her sister-in-law, was upset and angry at the thought that a daughter of hers was spreading lies.

The next day, the children went out as usual with their sheep. Lucia was sad because of her mother's attitude and walked in silence. Jacinta, too, was miserable and embarrassed because she had broken her promise. Yesterday's joy had turned to gloom because of the disbelief they had met. Yet, they could not get the words of the Lady out of their minds, especially the request for sacrifices. As they mulled over this problem, Francisco suggested they give their lunch to the sheep, and eat instead acorns, roots of bell flowers, mushrooms and similar unappetizing fare. As the days went by, they thought it would be more pleasing to the Lady to give their lunch to poor children instead of the sheep, which they proceeded to do.

But Lucia's biggest sacrifice was to face the anger of her mother. "This was all I needed for my old age," she lamented bitterly. "To think I always brought up my children to speak the truth. And now, this one brings me a whopper like this!"

And, as the days went by and the neighbors' gossip began to expose her to imagined ridicule, her frayed nerves caused her to add threats and scoldings to her efforts to break down Lucia's story. She even went so far as to beat her with the end of a broom. And when this failed, she marched the youngster up to the parish rectory in the hope that the awe and fear in which the children held the parish priest would melt her daughter's stubbornness.

When Lucia related this to her little friends, she said: "My mother wants me to contradict everything I said. But how can I?"

As June 13 drew near, the families of the children were looking forward to that day, which was the feast of St. Anthony of Padua, Patron Saint of Portugal, because of the festivities with which it was celebrated. But the children were preoccupied with other thoughts.

On the thirteenth, while happy crowds were heading for the open space in front of the village church, they were wending their way towards the Cova. Oddly enough, they were accompanied, not by members of their families, but by some fifty curious people who had come together from the different villages around. Having arrived at the Cova, Lucia, Francisco and Jacinta stood near the holmoak tree, while the others sat at ease, munching the loaves of bread they had brought in wicker baskets. They decided to say the Rosary.

They had hardly finished when Lucia's face lit up with animation. "Jacinta," she cried, "there comes Our Lady. There is the light."

The three children ran to the little tree that the Lady was pleased to use for a living pedestal, and there they beheld her again.

Lucia was heard to say: "Your Excellency told

me to come here; please say what you want of me." Then the bystanders began to hear something like a very faint voice, similar to the buzzing of a bee. Moreover, some of them noticed that the light of the sun seemed dimmer during the following minutes, though the sky was cloudless. Others said that the top of the tree, covered with new growth, appeared to bend and curve just before Lucia spoke, as if under a weight.

The Lady's reply to Lucia's question was, in Lucia's own words: "I want you to come here on the thirteenth day of the coming month, to recite five decades of the Rosary every day, and to learn to read. I will tell you later what I want."

Lucia then asked for the cure of a certain sick person.

"If he is converted, he will be cured during the year," was the reply.

"I should like to ask you to take us to Heaven," continued the child.

"Yes, Jacinta and Francisco I will take soon. But you must remain here for some time now. Jesus wishes to make use of you to have me acknowledged and loved. He wishes to establish in the world the devotion to my Immaculate Heart."

"I stay here, alone," cried Lucia in dismay.

"No, daughter. You are suffering very much, but do not be discouraged. I will never forsake you. My Immaculate Heart will be your refuge and the road that will lead you to God."

With these words, she opened her hands as on the previous occasion, and again communicated to them the light that streamed in two rays from her palms, enveloping the children in its heavenly radiance.

"In it we saw ourselves as if submerged in God," wrote Lucia later. "Jacinta and Francisco seemed to be in the part of this light that went up toward Heaven, and I in that part which spread itself over the ground. Before the palm of the right hand of Our Lady was a heart encircled by thorns which seemed to have pierced it like nails. We understood that it was the Immaculate Heart of Mary outraged by the sins of humanity, for which there must be reparation."

The Immaculate Heart of Mary! The Angel had said something about that. He had said: "Through the infinite merits of His Most Sacred Heart and the Immaculate Heart of Mary, I beg of You the conversion of sinners." Now the children saw both Jesus and Mary in that vision of the Most Blessed Trinity that enfolded them. Our Lady seemed neither sad nor joyful, but serious; but the impression left by the Word of God on the mind of Francisco, at any rate, was one of infinite sadness.

As this tremendous revelation faded from their view, the Lady, still surrounded by the light which emanated from her, arose without effort from the little tree and glided swiftly toward the East until she could be seen no longer. Some of the people standing around noticed that the new leaves on the top of the tree were drawn in the same direction, as if the Lady's garments had been trailed across them, and it was several hours before they gradually returned to their usual position.

Lucia remained looking at the vast emptiness of the sky. The people around her, though none of them had seen the Lady, realized that something extraordinary had occurred. Some started plucking leaves from the tree for relics or souvenirs. Finally, they began to disperse. A few, however, hung around seeking to glean some bit of information from the children. But they, dazed by this experience, found it was not easy to turn their thoughts to everyday affairs. As they took the road back to Aljustrel, they discouraged the last few importunate and inconsiderate questioners with: "It's a secret. We can't talk about it." Finally, the last of the strangers gave up and took themselves off, leaving them in peace.

Francisco had many questions of his own to ask when they were alone. As on the first occasion in May, he had seen all that Lucia and Jacinta had seen, but had heard nothing the Lady had said. He had to have everything explained to him by the two others and then was still puzzled about many details, especially about the reference to the Immaculate Heart.

Yes, he had seen the Heart and could not forget the rays of light from the Lady's hands, which he felt penetrating his own breast. "But why was the Lady with a heart in her hand," he persisted, "scattering over the world such a great light that is God? You were with Our Lady in the light I saw on the ground, Lucia. And Jacinta and I were going up toward the sky."

"It's this way," said Lucia. "You and Jacinta are going up to Heaven, and I am staying with the

Immaculate Heart of Mary some time longer on earth."

"How many years will you stay here?"

"I don't know. Plenty."

"Was it Our Lady who said so?"

"It was, and I saw it in the light that struck us in the breast."

"That's right," put in Jacinta, "I saw that, too."

When Lucia returned home after the second apparition, she came back to a mother whose physical ills, added to the imagined humiliation she was suffering (for she thought Lucia, with her silly story, was making fools of them all), had turned her into a very indignant and exasperated person. She had heard that fifty people had followed the children to the Cova da Iria. She knew now that the story was beyond recall. She feared to be considered a partner to her daughter's fabrication. The last straw was reached when Lucia made bold to ask her mother to send her to school to learn to read, as the Lady had requested.

"School indeed!" she expostulated. Then she added more quietly but more determinedly, "Tomorrow we are going again to the Pastor, and this time you are going to tell the truth."

The evening of that apparition, Lucia's sisters kept trying to learn the secret from her. Despite all attempts, however, they got nothing from her. Disappointed, they threatened all kinds of evil.

Frightened, Lucia went over to her cousins' home to warn them. "Tomorrow we will see the priest. I am going with my mother," Lucia said.

"My sisters have been trying to scare me," she added.

"We are going, too," Jacinta told her. "But my mother hasn't tried to scare us with any of those things. But if they do, we will suffer it for the love of Our Lord and for sinners."

Maria Rosa coached her daughter for the interview, saying: "Tell the priest that you lied so that on Sunday he can say in church that it was a lie and put an end to the whole thing."

The priest had already questioned Jacinta and Francisco. Now he compared the answers. Finally, he gave his decision. "It does not seem to be a revelation from Heaven," he said. "It may be a deception of the devil. We shall see. We shall see."

"The devil!" This was all Lucia needed to hear to make the misery within her almost unbearable. For days she was tormented by doubts. As time approached for the July meeting, she began to think her Pastor might be right after all. Finally, she sought out Jacinta and Francisco and told them: "I'm not going to the Cova anymore."

On the eve of the thirteenth, Lucia seemed determined to stick to her resolution. When she told Jacinta and Francisco, they became upset. Jacinta started to cry. Francisco sided with his sister. They could not imagine the devil impersonating Our Lady.

On the morning of the thirteenth, Lucia had suddenly come to the same conclusion. She ran to her cousins' house and found both of them kneeling by the bed, crying their eyes out. When they sensed Lucia had changed her mind, they jumped to their feet.

"Let's go," they said together, and in a jiffy were off.

This time, the crowd was much larger than previously. At the holmoak, Lucia led the Rosary, and when it was finished, she was heard to say: "Our Lady is coming!" A hush settled over the crowd, their eyes fixed on the children. They saw nothing and heard nothing.

But what transpired was the following:

Lucia asked the Lady: "What do you want of me?" "I want you to return on the thirteenth of next month. Continue to say the Rosary every day in honor of Our Lady of the Rosary to obtain peace for the world and the end of the war; for she alone can save it." To a question from Lucia, she replied: "Continue to come here every month. In October, I will tell you who I am and what I desire, and I will perform a miracle all shall see so that they may believe."

Then to remind the children of their special vocation and to inspire them to greater courage for the future, the Lady said: "Sacrifice yourselves for sinners; say often, especially when you make a sacrifice: 'My Jesus, it is for love of Thee, for the conversion of sinners and in reparation for the sins committed against the Immaculate Heart of Mary.' "

Then followed a vision of Hell, after which Our Lady explained: "You have seen Hell, where the souls of poor sinners go. To save them, God wants to establish throughout the world the devotion to my Immaculate Heart.

"If people will do what I tell you, many souls will be saved and there will be peace. The war is going to end. But if they do not stop offending God, another and worse war will break out in the reign of Pius XI. [Benedict XV was then Pope.] When you see a night illumined by an unknown light, know that it is the great sign God gives you that He is going to punish the world for its crimes by means of war, hunger, persecution of the Church and of the Holy Father.

"To forestall this, I shall come to ask the consecration of Russia to my Immaculate Heart and the Communion of Reparation on the First Saturdays.

"If they heed my requests, Russia will be converted, and there will be peace. If not, she shall spread her errors throughout the whole world, promoting wars and persecutions of the Church, the good will be martyred, the Holy Father will have much to suffer, various nations will be annihilated. [Russia had not yet fallen to Communism on July 13, 1917. This was not to occur until November 13, 1917.] In the end, my Immaculate Heart will triumph! The Holy Father will consecrate Russia to me, which will be converted, and some time of peace will be given to the world.

"In Portugal the dogma of the faith will be kept always."

"Do not tell this to anyone. To Francisco, yes, you may tell it."

To Lucia's question, "Do you want anything else from me?" Our Lady answered: "No, today I desire nothing else from you."

The impression this apparition made on the children was a turning point in their spiritual growth. All they could think of was to make sacrifices to keep sinners from going to Hell.

One day, as the cool hours of the morning gave way to stifling heat, they burned with thirst. Jacinta seemed happy that not a drop of water was near. "How good it is," she said. "I am thirsty, but I offer everything for the conversion of sinners."

Lucia, being the oldest, felt she should look after her cousins. So she went to a nearby house to fetch some water. When she returned, she offered it to Francisco. He said he didn't want to drink, saying he wanted to suffer for sinners. Jacinta likewise refused the water, saying, "I also want to offer a sacrifice." Lucia poured the water into the hollow of a rock for the sheep and then returned the empty jug to the house.

As the morning wore on, the heat, the crickets, the frogs and insects began to get on Jacinta's nerves. At one point, she cried out in desperation: "My head aches. Tell the crickets and the frogs to stop."

"Don't you want to suffer for sinners?" Lucia asked.

"Yes, Lucia, let them sing."

In August, the thirteenth was the feast of the Assumption, a Holy Day. But the children did not keep their appointment with the Lady because they were prevented by the magistrate of the County of Ourem, who was an anti-clerical Mason. He was upset at the growing popularity of the Cova da Iria and had decided to put a stop to the growing crowds that were flocking there. He summoned the parents of the children to the Pastor's residence and told them to bring the children with them. He pretended he wanted to see the miracle and insisted on taking the children to the Cova in his carriage. But, instead, he took them to Ourem and placed them in jail with common thieves and drunkards. He wanted the children to reveal the secrets to him so that he could expose the whole thing as a hoax. But despite all his wiles, the children remained firm in their refusal to answer his questions. Finally, in desperation, he threatened to put them in a caldron of boiling oil, one by one. But the children preferred to die rather than to betray Our Lady's confidence. Finally, seeing himself defeated, he gave up and returned the children to Aljustrel.

On the following Sunday, the 19th of August, Lucia, Francisco and his elder brother John left for Valinhos, not far away, where they intended to spend the afternoon.

About four o'clock, Lucia became aware of the signs that usually preceded the apparitions of Our Lady. But, Jacinta was not there. So she tried to persuade John to call his sister. But he seemed reluctant to do so, so she bribed him with a few pennies, and off he went. Not finding her at home, he tracked her down at her godmother's house and quickly whispered the news to her. They raced together to Valinhos. As they reached the field, a flash rent the air. And there, over another holmoak, the Lady appeared in all her beauty.

"What do you want of me?" Lucia asked.

"I want you to continue to come to the Cova da Iria on the thirteenth and to continue to say the Rosary every day."

Lucia then asked Our Lady if she would be willing to perform a miracle so that all might believe.

"Yes," Our Lady answered. "In the last month, October, I shall perform a miracle so that all may believe in my apparitions. If they had not taken you to the village, the miracle would have been greater. St. Joseph will come with the Baby Jesus to give peace to the world. Our Lord also will come to bless the people. Besides, Our Lady of the Rosary and Our Lady of Sorrows will come. Pray, pray a good deal, for many souls go to Hell for not having someone to pray and make sacrifices for them."

Then, the Lady took leave of her little friends, rising toward the East as before.

John, of course, had seen nothing. He watched disappointed as the children broke off a small branch which the robe of Our Lady had touched.

John and Lucia stayed at Valinhos with their sheep, while Francisco and Jacinta rushed home with their precious branch to tell their parents of the unexpected visit of Our Lady. They passed Lucia's house and related what had happened to Maria Rosa, who detected a very pleasant odor coming from the branch. Then Jacinta took the branch to her father and mother, who also noted the special fragrance of the branch.

The plea of Our Lady, to pray and make sacrifices for sinners to keep them from Hell, thereafter never left the minds of the children. They were more eager than ever to make sacrifices. For hours on end they said the prayer the Angel had taught them. They went for days without drinking anything. Indeed, they went the whole month of August without water.

One day, they passed by a pond. Jacinta was overcome with thirst and was tempted to drink from it. It was dirty water that animals drank from and people even did their washing in. Though Lucia tried to dissuade her, Jacinta said, "I'll drink this and offer the Lord the sacrifice of drinking this foul water instead of my thirst."

Another day, Jacinta's mother gave them a bunch of grapes to munch on. Jacinta said: "As a sacrifice, let's not eat them." Just then, they saw some children on the road and ran to give them the luscious-looking grapes. On another occasion, Olimpia gave Jacinta a basket of figs for the three of them. Instead of eating her share, Jacinta ran off so as not to be tempted to eat them.

Again, another day, Jacinta hurt herself in some nettles. She was happy to find a new form of mortification. Another occasion to offer sacrifices for sinners came when they found a piece of rope. Lucia tied it around her arm and soon discovered that it hurt. The rope was thick and rough. They cut it into three pieces and tied it around their waists. They even wore the rope to bed, which prevented them from getting the rest they needed.

The thirteenth of September finally came. Crowds of people, divided between believers and unbelievers, streamed in the direction of the Cova.

The children made their way there with difficulty. When they arrived at the holmoak, they started the Rosary. In a few moments, Our Lady appeared as usual.

Lucia began by asking: "What do you want of me?"

"Let the people continue to say the Rosary to attain the end of the war." Then she repeated the promise she had made in the last apparition, but added: "God is pleased with your sacrifices but does not want you to sleep with the rope. Wear it only during the day."

Lucia pleaded, "Please, perform a miracle that all may believe."

"Yes, in October I will perform a miracle that all may believe."

With that, she began to leave, gliding toward the East as usual.

Word soon got around that Our Lady had promised to work a miracle in October. The news spread like wildfire throughout the country. People came from miles away on October 13th. The weather was bad for travelling on foot as most of them did. It rained, and there was a raw wind that chilled the travelers to the bone. It has been estimated that the crowd at the Cova da Iria numbered at least 70,000 persons.

It was with the greatest difficulty that the children made their way to the holmoak. As usual, the Rosary was said. At the appointed time, Our Lady appeared. And, as usual, Lucia asked: "What do you want of me?"

"I want to tell you that they must build a chapel

here in my honor, that I am the Lady of the Rosary, that they [must] continue to say the Rosary every day. The War will end and the soldiers will return to their homes soon."

"I have some favors to ask," Lucia replied. "Do you wish to grant them or not?"

"Some I will! Others I will not! They must amend their lives, ask forgiveness for their sins, offend not Our Lord anymore," Our Lady continued, her face becoming very grave, "for He is already much offended."

"Do you wish anything else from me?" the girl asked.

"I desire nothing else," was the reply.

As Our Lady took leave of the children, she opened her hands and emitted a flood of light. While she was rising she pointed toward the sun, and the light gleaming from her hands brightened the sun itself.

Lucia and her cousins looked at the sun, now as pale as the moon. To the left of the sun, St. Joseph emerged from the bright clouds, visible only to his waist, sufficient to allow him to raise his right hand and to make, together with the Child Jesus, whom he held, the Sign of the Cross three times over the world. Our Lady stood to the right of the sun, dressed in the blue and white robes of Our Lady of the Rosary. Lucia alone saw what followed. She saw Our Lord, dressed as the Divine Redeemer, like St. Joseph visible only from the chest up, blessing the world. Beside Him, Our Lady was dressed now in the purple robes of Our Lady of Sorrows, but without the sword. Finally,

Our Lady appeared again, only to Lucia, clothed in the simple brown robes of Our Lady of Mount Carmel.

Meanwhile, the crowd was witnessing what was called "The Miracle of the Sun." The sun had taken on an extraordinary color. It could be looked at with ease. At a certain point, the sun seemed to be whirling or "dancing," as people later said, until it seemed to loosen itself from the sky and fall upon the people.

The people cried out with one voice, fearing the End of the World had come. When the spectacular display was over—it lasted about ten minutes—they discovered that their clothes were perfectly dry; whereas, before they had been soaking wet.

As Our Lady had promised, she took the children of Ti Marto and Olimpia to Heaven fairly soon after the events described above. Francisco was the first to be called to Heaven. Late in October, 1918, World War I was within a few months of becoming part of the history of wars. About the same time, there was spreading over Europe and America, an influenza epidemic that decimated thousands of homes. Few places were to escape its ravages, for it found its way even into the remote hamlets of the Serra da Aire. Whole families came down with the "flu." In the Marto home, every member was laid low, except the father. Francisco was the hardest hit. And he was the first of the three Fatima seers to die. After a lingering illness, during which he suffered much, he died on Friday, April 4, 1919.

Part II

THE STORY OF JACINTA

It was hardly to be expected that, after the apparitions, the three little children should enjoy the privacy and intimacy of their own company in the same undisturbed way as when they had first begun to tend their sheep. Whatever privacy and seclusion they obtained had to be wrested from the people who were continually seeking them out, sometimes almost with violence. That is, they deliberately had to avoid visitors, when they could, usually through some simple little stratagem, or by hiding away like brigands down by the well in the back of Lucia's property or among the huge protecting rocks of the Cabeco Cave.

But, of course, as time went on, they found it increasingly difficult to escape from the curious and the seekers of favors, and more often than not, they had to put up with these inevitable annoyances as part of the sufferings they had promised to endure for the conversion of sinners.

There was a story making the rounds, for instance, of a poor woman who had thrown herself on her knees before Jacinta, crying and begging her to obtain from Our Lady her cure of a painful infirmity. Jacinta had taken the poor woman by the hands and tried to raise her. Proving too weak for this, the child knelt down beside her and prayed for her. Later, the woman returned to the Cova, cured and grateful to Our Lady.

Another time, a soldier came, crying like a child, to recommend himself to the prayers of the little children. He had been called to war, and had a sick wife and three young children at home.

"Don't cry," said Jacinta, "Our Lord is so good!"

The little shepherds prayed for the soldier and added an Ave Maria for him to their daily beads.

At the end of a few months, the man came back with his wife and children to thank Our Lady. His prayer had been doubly granted. On the eve of his departure, he had been stricken with a sudden fever, and had been sent home on an unlimited furlough. And soon his wife had found herself cured, as he declared, "by a real miracle of Our Lady."

There was a woman in the parish who used to insult the seers whenever she met them. One day, as she tumbled out of a tavern, quite tipsy, she added blows to the usual insults.

When they had escaped from her, Jacinta said: "We must pray hard to Our Lady for the conversion of that woman and make sacrifices for her. She says so many sinful things, and such terribly bad things, that if she does not confess them she will go to Hell."

A few days later, the two little girls were playing tag, and happened to pass the vixen's house. Jacinta stopped suddenly and said to Lucia: "Let's stop playing! It will be a sacrifice for the conversion of sinners."

And, without thinking that she might be seen, she joined her hands, raised her eyes to Heaven, and recited the formula of offering. The poor woman was watching the children through the little window in her house. She was so much won by Jacinta's prayer that she stopped insulting them, asked them to pray for her, and became a fervent petitioner at the Cova da Iria.

Sister Lucia relates in her *Memoirs* another remarkable incident. An aunt of Lucia, living at Fatima, had a son who had left home and was never heard from. The aunt came to see her niece to ask her to pray for the prodigal. Lucia was away, however, so the request was presented to Jacinta.

After a few days, the young man returned and begged his parent's pardon. On his way home at night, he said, he had got lost in the mountains and woods, and a violent storm had blown up. Thoroughly frightened, he had fallen on his knees imploring God's mercy, when suddenly he saw his cousin Jacinta beside him. She had given him her hand and had led him to the road, then left him, after pointing in the direction he was to go.

When explanations were asked of Jacinta, she answered: "I don't even know where those forests or those mountains are. But I prayed hard to Our Lady for him, because of Aunt Victoria's sorrow."

"How all that happened," said Sister Lucia, "I don't know, but God knows."

When Francisco fell ill with the flu, as I mentioned earlier, Jacinta followed him only a few days later. In fact, as we know, all of the family was stricken except Ti Marto, the father.

One day, Lucia came to see Jacinta and found her strangely elated. "Look, Lucia!" she said, "Our Lady came to see us here, and she said that she is coming very soon to take Francisco to Heaven. And she asked me if I still wanted to convert more sinners and I said, 'Yes.'

"Our Lady wants me to go to two hospitals. But not to be cured. It is to suffer more for the love of God, for the conversion of sinners and in reparation for the offenses committed against the Immaculate Heart of Mary.

"She said that you were not going," she continued. "She said my mother is going to take me, and then I will stay there alone."

Now, this is hardly the kind of news ordinarily calculated to bring happiness to the recipient. It is, then, an indication of the remarkable progress in the spiritual life the children had made—to see them look forward to suffering with joy rather than sadness. Let us make no mistake, the children did not love suffering in itself. Pain was just as unpleasant to them as it is to us. But the fruit of their suffering—reparation to the Immaculate Heart of Mary and the conversion of sinners—was a motive now so overpowering that it eclipsed the natural aversion to pain which they shared with all human beings. It was the good they could accomplish through their sufferings that attracted them. By contrast, it is eloquent of the feebleness of our own response to this same supernatural appeal when we find ourselves making so much of the slightest sacrifice and striving to avoid every form of suffering, often with a zeal worthy of a better cause.

During their illness, the little brother and sister occupied adjoining rooms. Often, Jacinta would listen until she felt sure that both her parents were out of the house. Then she would slip out of bed and steal into Francisco's room to perch beside him and talk, until this was discovered and forbidden. Toward evening, Lucia usually would stop in on her way home from school.

"Well, Jacinta," she would say: "have you made many sacrifices today?"

"Yes, a lot," the little girl would answer. "My mother was out and I wanted to go many times to visit Francisco, and I didn't do it."

Lucia might tell of some sacrifices she had performed during the day.

"I did that too," Jacinta would speak up. "I love Our Lord and Our Lady and I never get tired of telling them that I love them. When I tell that to them, it seems sometimes that I have a fire burning in my breast, a fire that does not consume. . .Oh, how I would like to be able to go again to the hills to say the Rosary in the cave. But I can't anymore. When you go to the Cova da Iria, pray for me, Lucia! I'm sure I'll never go there again. Now you go to Francisco's room because I want to make the sacrifice of being alone."

Being the mother of such heroic and saintly

children did not necessarily make the lot of Olimpia any easier, and her heart unquestionably was subjected to a great strain as she overheard them speaking so assuredly of their imminent deaths. In fact, it was conceivably harder for her to sit by and not be called upon for the sympathy a mother's heart was made to lavish on sick little ones. There is possibly a hint of this in what Olimpia told Father De Marchi, on being questioned for information concerning the children during their illness. "It made me sad," she said, "to watch Jacinta in bed, covering her face with her hands and not moving for hours at a time. She said she was thinking. When I asked her what she was thinking about, she smiled and said, 'Nothing, Mother.' She kept no secrets, however, from her cousin Lucia. Lucia brought joy and happiness to everyone. When the two girls were alone, they talked continually and in such a way that none of us could catch a word of what they said, no matter how hard we tried. When anyone went near them, they lowered their heads and kept quiet. No one could penetrate their mysterious confidences."

"What did Jacinta tell you?" Olimpia once asked Lucia, as she was leaving for her home. Lucia merely smiled and sped away. "But I know," continued Olimpia, "that they used to say Rosary after Rosary, at least seven or eight every day and there was no end to their short prayers."

When it was obvious to everyone that the end was near for Francisco, Jacinta slipped out of her bed to entrust him with a message for Heaven. "Give my compliments to Our Lord and Our

Lady," she said. "Tell them I shall suffer all they want for sinners and to make reparation to the Immaculate Heart of Mary."

After his death, the separation from her beloved brother, beloved playmate, and beloved partner in the revelations from Our Lady, was in itself about as great a suffering as Jacinta had to bear. Despite the fact that she gamely offered it up, her loneliness was nonetheless acute. She missed her brother terribly.

She confided once to Lucia: "I'm thinking of Francisco. How much I would love to see him. But I think also of the war that is going to come. So many people will die and so many will go to Hell. Many cities will be burned to the ground, and many priests will be killed. Look, Lucia, I'm going to Heaven. But when you see that night illuminated by that strange light, you also run away to Heaven."

"Don't you see it's impossible to run away to Heaven?" Lucia said.

"Yes, you can't do that. But don't be afraid. I'll pray a lot for you in Heaven, and for the Holy Father also, and for Portugal, for the war not to come here, and for all priests."

Lucia often tried to brighten the sick girl's room with flowers picked from the Serra. Sometimes she would bring them from the Cova, or again from Valinhos, but the best ones were from the slope of the Cabeco. Like as not, however, the flowers would remind Jacinta of these favorite spots and fill her with a little sadness because she would not see these places again. She once said to Lucia: "I'll never go over there to Cabeco again, nor to Valinhos, nor to the Cova da Iria! And I am so sorry!"

"But what does it matter to you?" Lucia responded. "You are going to Heaven, to see Our Lord and Our Lady."

"That's true," she answered. And the thought made her happy again.

One of her most ardent desires was to receive Holy Communion. Once, a cousin of hers gave her a picture representing a chalice and a host. She took it, kissed it tenderly, and said, "It is the hidden Jesus. I love Him so! Who will let me receive Him in church? Is there Communion in Heaven? If there is, I shall go every day. If the Angel came to the hospital to bring me Holy Communion a second time, how happy I should be!"

When Lucia came back from church after having received Communion, Jacinta would make her come quite close so that she might feel the Divine Presence. She would sometimes say: "I don't know how it is. I feel Our Lord within me. I understand what He says to me without seeing Him or hearing Him. But how sweet it is to be with Him!"

Someone had given Lucia a picture of the Sacred Heart. She gave it to Jacinta, who kept it constantly, and often kissed it.

"I am kissing," she would say, "the Heart of Him whom I love above all. I wish I also had a picture of the Heart of Mary. I would be so pleased to have the two together."

On the occasion of another visit, she confided

to Lucia: "It won't be long before I go to Heaven. You, Lucia, will remain on earth to spread the news that Our Lord wants the whole world to have devotion to the Immaculate Heart of Mary. When you have to speak, don't hide yourself. Tell the whole world that God wants to grant His graces through the mediation of the Immaculate Heart of Mary; that we must not hesitate to ask them through her; that the Heart of Jesus wants to be venerated along with the Immaculate Heart of Mary; that men must ask the Immaculate Heart for peace, because God has confided it to her. If I could only put into all hearts what I feel here within me, what makes me love the Hearts of Jesus and Mary so!"

Father Fonseca, in his book *Our Lady of Light*, describes the visits of others to Jacinta besides Lucia. Sometimes some of the village children would come to see her, but oddly enough, she preferred only those who were younger than herself. These she taught prayers and hymns. If able to, she would play with them, sitting on her bed, or else on the floor in the middle of the room. Then she would make them say their beads and advise them never to offend Our Lord so as not to go to Hell.

Some children would spend a whole morning or a whole afternoon with her. But "when they had gone," says Lucia, "they didn't dare come back, as if respect kept them away. They would come for me and ask me to introduce them. Others waited in front of the door till my aunt or Jacinta would call them and ask them to come in."

The women of the village also liked to come and spend some time with her. One who has been to Aljustrel knows how almost inevitable it was that everyone in this tiny hamlet should have, at some time or other, dropped in on each other for a visit. The doors of the homes are always open and so close to the road that one could almost visit right from there.

The village women often brought their sewing or knitting and would sit by Jacinta's bed working and talking. Others might come from a distance, eager to ask a million questions. Their intentions were good, of course. But who hasn't lain in a sick bed, tired and longing for nothing more than a little peace and quiet, and wishing one's talkative visitors were a thousand miles away. Poor Jacinta was not immune from such visitors, as she revealed when she said to Lucia one day: "My head aches from hearing those people. Now I can't run away or hide myself, so I have more sacrifices to offer Our Lord."

Jacinta's sickness showed no signs of loosening its hold on her. On the contrary, the influenza turned into pleurisy and an abscess formed on her side. Her mother felt so sad to see her in such pain, but Jacinta always came back with a consoling word: "Don't worry, Mother, for I'm going to Heaven. I'll pray a lot for you there. Don't cry. I'm all right . . ."

But before she could go to Heaven, the Lady had revealed to her that she must first spend some time in *two* hospitals. The time had arrived for this prophecy to come true.

It was a sad journey for poor Ti Marto the day he took his sick Jacinta to the hospital of St. Augustine in the town of Ourem. The little girl clung tightly to the small burro as they made their way slowly along the road, which is practically all down hill right from Fatima to Ourem. It was the doctor who had insisted on hospital care for the sick child, and though Ti Marto's resources were meager, he was ready to make any sacrifice to restore his beloved little pet to health, especially now that Francisco was gone. Jacinta, who knew already that her father's hopes were doomed to frustration, nevertheless consented to go because the Lady had informed her that before she would be taken to Heaven, she must first spend some time in two hospitals. This, then, was one of the signs she had been expecting.

In spite of this, and in spite of her willingness to sacrifice herself for the conversion of sinners and in reparation for the offenses committed against the Immaculate Heart of Mary, the whole thing remained a cross which human nature found it hard to bear. Her eyes had been filled with tears a few moments ago when she had embraced Lucia and whispered to her: "Lucia, if only you could come with me! The hardest thing to me is to have to go without you. Maybe the hospital is very dark, where we can't see a thing! And I'll be there suffering alone."

As she had feared, Jacinta's greatest cross turned out to be her loneliness. Actually, Ourem was only a few miles away from home. But, as I have indicated already, the journey involved for anyone who went there a long tiresome climb on foot in returning to Aljustrel. It meant a whole day away from home and work. As a result, her only visitors during the two months she was there were her mother and Lucia, who came to see her one day. Olimpia took advantage of the occasion to do a little shopping, but Lucia spent the whole time at the side of her sick friend. These must have been golden hours for both of them, hours in which they must have re-lived the precious moments spent with Francisco at the well and at the Cabeco. Lucia, in her *Memoirs*, lifts the veil of secrecy only enough to tell us that she found Jacinta as happy as always to suffer for the love of God and the Immaculate Heart of Mary, for the conversion of sinners and for the Holy Father. "That was her ideal," she says. "That was all she spoke about."

Even though they remained together two days, this visit must have seemed to them all too short. The very joy they had felt in being reunited must have made the parting all the harder. Once more the clouds of solitude shut out the sunshine from Jacinta's room. The loneliness returned. And her physical condition showed no signs of improvement. The abscess in her side was worse than ever, so much so, that the doctor finally admitted that the lack of improvement did not warrant continuing the expense of hospital care. Therefore, late in August—it was 1919—she was sent home again.

Father Formigao, one of the first priests to believe in the apparitions, went to visit her at home about this time. He writes: "She was all bones, and it was a shock to see how thin her arms were. She was running a fever all the time. Pneumonia, then tuberculosis and pleurisy ate away her strength. I remembered, as I saw her, that Our Lady had promised Bernadette of Lourdes that she too would not be happy in this world, but in the next. I wondered if Our Lady made the same promise to Jacinta."

Jacinta's weakness now created a problem for her that she decided to share with Lucia. "When I'm alone," she told her, "I get out of bed to say the Angel's prayer. But now, I can't bow my head to the floor any more because I fall; I say it on my knees."

Lucia didn't feel equal to solving this problem herself so she took it to the Pastor of Olival, who was always kind to her. He advised her immediately, of course, to tell Jacinta to say her prayers in bed.

"But will Our Lord like it?" Jacinta asked when informed of his answer.

"Yes, He will," said Lucia. "Our Lord wants us to do what the priest says."

"Then it's all right. I won't get up any more for my prayers."

There were times when the little girl showed a slight, temporary improvement. Her one desire then would be to be permitted to go to the Cova. Her parents would not listen to this, but she did prevail upon them sometimes to allow her to go to Mass. She actually wanted to go every morning. But Lucia would counsel her: "Don't come to Mass, it is too much for you. Besides, today isn't Sunday."

"That doesn't matter," she would reply. "I want to go in place of the sinners who don't go, even on Sundays. . . Look, Lucia, do you know? Our Lord is so sad, and Our Lady told us that He must not be offended any more. He is already offended too much, and no one pays any attention to it. They keep committing the same sins."

"Have you performed any sacrifices, Jacinta?"

"Yes, Lucia. Last night, I was very thirsty, but I didn't drink anything. I felt a lot of pain, and I offered Our Lord the sacrifice of not turning in bed. That is why I couldn't sleep."

One day, Jacinta's mother brought her a glass of milk. "You drink this down, Jacinta; it's good for you."

"I don't want it, Mother," she replied, pushing the glass away. Olimpia insisted, but Jacinta would not give in.

"I don't know how I am going to make her take anything," her mother said as she walked away.

Lucia, who was present, apparently didn't agree with Jacinta. "How is it," she said to her, "that you disobey your mother! Aren't you going to offer that sacrifice to Our Lord?"

Jacinta's sensitive conscience was quick to respond. Her eyes immediately filled with tears. She called her mother back and asked her pardon. "I'll take anything you want me to take, Mother," she now said. Her mother brought back the glass of milk, and she took it without showing any signs of revulsion. But afterwards she confided to Lucia: "If you only knew how hard it was for me to drink it."

Henceforth, she needed no further reminders to use such opportunities to do penance for sinners. Another time, her mother, who knew she loved grapes, brought her a bunch with her milk. But Jacinta pushed the grapes aside and just drank the milk. And again, we learn from Lucia the interior struggle this gesture involved, for Jacinta later told her: "I did want the grapes so much and it was so hard for me to drink that milk. But I preferred to offer a sacrifice."

About the middle of January, Jacinta had another visitor, whose company she preferred even to Lucia's. It was Our Lady, who appeared to her again to inform her that the time was soon coming for her to visit the second hospital.

Jacinta revealed the whole thing to Lucia. "Lucia," she said, "Our Lady told me that I'm going to go to another hospital in Lisbon and that I'll never see you again or my parents and that after suffering a great deal, I shall die alone. She said that I should not be afraid since she will come to take me with her to Heaven."

But at nine, it's hard not to be afraid, even when the Queen of Heaven reassures you. So she began to sob as she embraced Lucia tightly to her: "I will never see you again. Pray a lot for me, for I am going to die alone."

This thought seemed to prey on her mind. Another day, Lucia found her embracing a picture of Our Lady, praying aloud: "My dear little Mother, so I am going to die alone?"

Lucia, attempting to cheer her up, said: "Why do you worry about dying alone? What do you care, when Our Lady herself is going to come for you?"

"It's true. I don't care. I don't know why, but sometimes I forget that she is going to come for me."

"Take heart, Jacinta. You have only a little while to wait before you go to Heaven. As for me. . ." She left the sentence unfinished.

Now it was Jacinta's turn to console Lucia.

"Poor thing. Don't cry, Lucia, I shall pray a lot in Heaven for you. You are going to stay here, but it is Our Lady who wants it."

"Jacinta, what are you going to do in Heaven?"

"I'm going to love Jesus a lot, and the Immaculate Heart of Mary, and pray and pray for you, for the Holy Father, my parents, brothers, sisters, and for everyone who has asked me, and for sinners."

Not long after Our Lady's visit, Father Formigao came to see Jacinta in the company of Doctor and Mrs. Enrico Lisboa. Father De Marchi gives the doctor's own account of how this came about.

"Around the middle of January, 1920," the doctor stated, "we stopped at Santarem to see Father Formigao, who could inform us better than anyone else of the events that had taken place at Fatima. We went to the Cova da Iria with him and said the Rosary. Returning to Fatima, we stopped in to see Jacinta. She was pale and thin and walked with great difficulty. Her family was not upset about her condition, as the only ambition of Jacinta was to go to Our Lady. I reproached them for not doing all in their power to help the girl. They answered that it was useless, as Our Lady wanted to take her away and that she had already been at the hospital at Ourem, and nothing could be done. I told them that the will of Our Lady is above human resources and that to make sure that Our Lady really wanted to take her, they should go to all lengths to save her.

"My words disturbed them, so they asked the priest for his advice. He confirmed my words. Thus Jacinta came to Lisbon on the second of February, 1920, where she was placed under the care of one of the leading specialists on children's diseases."

Before leaving for Lisbon, however, Jacinta got her mother to take her for the last time to the Cova da Iria. "I decided to take Jacinta there on the donkey," Olimpia tells us, "with the help of one of my friends. The child was so weak that she could not even stand. As we went by the bog of Carreira, Jacinta got down from the donkey and began to say the Rosary alone. Then she picked some flowers to adorn the little Chapel. When we reached the Cova, we all knelt and she prayed for a while in her own way. After she got up, she said, 'When Our Lady went away, she passed over those trees and entered Heaven so fast that it seemed as if her feet were caught in the door.' "

There was one more sad task to fulfill, to take leave of Lucia, whom she knew she would never see again. Since Francisco's death, she had leaned more and more on Lucia, looking forward to her company as her greatest pleasure. Being the only two on earth to share the Lady's secret had made them one in a way that transcended all natural relationships and bound them closer together than even the ties of blood ever could have. It was a much greater wrench, then, for the little girl to part from Lucia than from her own parents. "She kept her arms around me for a long time," Lucia writes in her *Memoirs*. "She was crying and saying to me, 'Never again shall we see each other. Pray a great deal for me, for I am going to Heaven. There I will pray a lot for you. Don't ever tell anyone the secret, even if they kill you. Love Jesus a great deal and the Immaculate Heart of Mary. Make many sacrifices for sinners.'"

Once again, Jacinta began the descent from her beloved Fatima toward Ourem and Lisbon. This time she was accompanied by her mother and her brother Antonio. The journey was much longer, for they had to go beyond Ourem to the little town of Chao de Macas to get the train to Lisbon.

According to the arrangements that had been made, a rich family of Lisbon had been asked to receive the little patient until she was admitted to the hospital. But on seeing the real state of the child, they refused to take her into their home. There was in Lisbon, however, a person looking for just such an opportunity. It was Mother Maria da Purificacao Godinho who, with a few other secularized Franciscan nuns, ran a little orphanage on the Rua da Estrela, the highest point in Lisbon. She had heard the story of Fatima and was anxious to go there, when providentially, it came to her attention that Jacinta herself was in Lisbon and in need of a home. She welcomed the little girl to the orphanage with the real charity of the poor and could not thank Our Lady enough for the honor.

The home was adjacent to a little chapel called Our Lady of the Miracles, and as a matter of fact, a door and little balcony opened into the chapel from the second floor of the orphanage. When Jacinta became aware of this arrangement, she was filled with joy. She hadn't expected the happiness of living in the same house with Jesus. This feature made up for many of the sorrows that leaving Fatima had caused her, and, added to the bighearted hospitality of Mother Godinho, it made even saying good-bye to her own mother, a few days later, easier than she had hoped.

Across from the orphanage was Estrela Park, colorful with its flower-lined paths, its roaming peacocks and, on Sundays, with the parade of hundreds of people gaily strolling along. Weekdays, the people had to work and so the park was quieter, and Jacinta loved to sit by the little balcony onto which her private room opened up. From there she would admire the beauties of nature that, more often than not, served as stepping stones to the contemplation of the beautiful world of the supernatural that Our Lady had opened up to her. What she liked best of all, however, was to be taken to the other little balcony, the one that opened out onto the chapel. Here she would sit and commune with the hidden Jesus, or say one Rosary after another.

Yes, the Cova was far away and she would never see it again. But here was Jesus, and that made up for it. Not only that, but the beautiful Lady who had made the Cova so dear to her, she was here too at times, as Mother Godinho discovered one day to her joy when the little patient calmly requested her to move over a little from the foot of the bed, because, as she said: "Mother dear, I am expecting Our Lady."

The last trial little Jacinta had to face, of dying alone in the hospital at Lisbon, undoubtedly was one of the greatest Our Lady asked her to undergo. Yet, we can see now, what perhaps Jacinta herself could not see then, that this arrangement was very providential, since it brought her into contact with Mother Godinho, who lovingly treasured every word and action of the little seer and who gathered them together like precious jewels for the benefit of posterity.

It goes without saying that Mother Godinho considers the few weeks that Jacinta spent in her little orphanage as the most wonderful days of her life, and it was evident to visitors that the joy of them had not yet left her. I was myself privileged (See Part III, "A Trip to Fatima") to spend several hours with her in the very room where Jacinta had stayed. Father Louis Gonzaga de Oliveira, our kind host in Lisbon, was a very close friend of Mother Godinho, and he took us to see her on two occasions. As soon as he indicated to her that we had come all the way from America to visit Fatima, her face broke into a motherly smile that revealed immediately how pleased she was. And she needed no further encouragement to begin to speak of Jacinta and the days the little girl had spent in her home.

Mother Godinho was a very plain, peasant sort of looking woman. She was short, rather squat, with thick lips and very few teeth. By American standards she was not impressive. The temptation to make much of such physical defects as hers, however, was quickly overcome by the realization that in Europe the struggle for the essentials of life was so great that often little time or thought could be spared for non-essentials.

In fact, one listening to Mother Godinho talk on and on with great affection of the days of grace when Jacinta had been in that room—and, at times, Our Lady, too—could not help but wonder if maybe we in America with all our latest advances in hygiene and soft living are as well off as we think we are—that is, if part of the price we have paid for these material and physical benefits is an estrangement from things of the spirit. I'm sure Mother Godinho would not have traded places with anyone in America. I know that she loved the poor and simple little home where she struggled to provide for her charges.

The air may be somewhat stale, the furniture stiff and old-fashioned, yet Our Lady appeared there. That makes everything in that place not only acceptable but sacred.

It is not difficult to understand, therefore, why I considered it such a privilege to be there that Sunday in May, to sit and listen to the woman speak who had tended little Jacinta, to have pointed out for us the spot where the bed had stood, where Our Lady had probably stood. All this filled me with an awe that could only be expressed in sacred silence. I might have asked Father de Oliveira—acting as our interpreter, since Mother Godinho spoke no English—to put special questions to her and try to elicit more information about Jacinta. But I was not inclined to. I felt inclined only to sit and to wonder at the goodness of God, who in His Divine Providence had arranged this visit for me. And this feeling of wonder grew to the point where it almost overwhelmed me when Mother Godinho, without any solicitation on my part, placed in my hands the little blue dress friends of Jacinta had made for her to wear during the apparitions, and a little white undergarment that went with it. I remember sitting with those garments in my lap and listening to Mother Godinho relate as effortlessly as if it had all happened yesterday that chapter of the Story of Fatima in which she herself figured so prominently.

The climax came when she took out for our inspection a box of relics. She showed us the little jackknife that had belonged to Jacinta and with which she cut her bread. She showed us a little bottle in which were the remains of the last roll Jacinta had attempted to eat before going to the hospital. The remains of the roll were nothing but loose crumbs now. I impulsively touched them with my finger and put the few crumbs that adhered to my finger to my mouth. Maybe it was this gesture, obviously indicative of my great respect, that made Mother Godinho top off the afternoon for me with an almost unbelievable gift.

She had in her hands the portion that remains of the brown head-covering little Jacinta had worn during the first apparition. She passed it around and we all touched it. Then she took her scissors and smilingly cut a two-inch portion from it. She handed it to me. I was overjoyed. In my mind, I quickly calculated that even after it was divided into four pieces—one for each of us priests—that which remained for each of us would be a generous portion indeed of so precious a relic. But I was almost floored a moment later, when I saw Mother Godinho cut three small pieces from the original for the other priests and indicated that the piece she had given me was all for me.

Mother Godinho had preserved fresh in her memory many of the things Jacinta said to her during her last few weeks on earth. And it is obvious to anyone who reads these remarks that they could have been inspired, if not actually revealed, only by Our Lady herself. For they manifest a maturity of judgment that ordinarily would be far beyond that of a nine-year-old child.

Jacinta did not hesitate to "preach" to some of the little girls in the home. "It was funny to listen to her," Mother Godinho good-naturedly remarked. She told one little girl one day, "You must never tell a lie or be lazy, but be very obedient. Do everything well and with patience for the love of Our Lord, if you want to go to Heaven!"

Mother Godinho used to like to sit by her side at the window that looked out upon Estrela Park and engage her in conversation. Her mature remarks and heavenly wisdom impressed her so much that she asked Jacinta one day who had taught her all these things. She answered: "Our Lady taught me, but some things I think out myself. I like to think very much."

Here are some of her statements, according to Mother Godinho.

"Our Lady said that there are many wars and discords in the world. Wars are only punishments for the sins of the world. Our Lady cannot stay the arm of her Beloved Son upon the world anymore. It is necessary to do penance. If the people amend themselves, Our Lord shall still come to the aid of the world. If they do not amend themselves, punishment shall come. . . If men do not amend their lives, Almighty God will send the world, beginning with Spain, a punishment such as never has been." She then spoke of "great world events that were to take place around the year 1940." However, she did not elaborate, since this was part of the secret relating to World War II that she could not reveal. As we know now, Sister Lucia received permission to make this part of the secret known, in 1927.

Here are some of Jacinta's other comments that Mother Godinho has preserved for us.

"My dear Mother, the sins that bring most souls to Hell are the sins of the flesh. Certain fashions are going to be introduced which will offend Our Lord very much. Those who serve God should not follow these fashions. The Church has no fashions: Our Lord is always the same.

"Many marriages," she remarked, "are not good; they do not please Our Lord and are not of God."

In another vein, she continued: "Pray a great deal for governments. Pity those governments which persecute the religion of Our Lord. If the governments left the Church in peace and gave liberty to our Holy Religion, they would be blessed by God."

Addressing herself directly to Mother Godinho, she once said: "My good Mother, do not give yourself to immodest clothes. Run away from riches. Love holy poverty and silence very much. Be very charitable, even with those who are unkind. Never criticize others and avoid those who do.

"Confession is a Sacrament of mercy. That is why people should approach the confessional with confidence and joy.

"The Mother of God wants a larger number of virgin souls to bind themselves to her by the vow of chastity. I would enter a convent with great joy, but my joy is greater because I am going to Heaven. To be a religious, one has to be very pure in soul and in body."

"And do you know what it means to be pure?" Mother Godinho asked.

"Yes, I do. To be pure in body means to preserve chastity. To be pure in soul means to avoid sin, not to look at what would be sinful, not to steal, never to lie and always to tell the truth, even when it is hard."

Knowing that these remarks were inspired directly or indirectly by Our Lady herself, and are not just the wise sayings of a precocious child, we who are privileged to hear them will find it hard to put together an excuse good enough to exempt us from giving them very serious consideration.

The last sign Jacinta was looking for on the highway to Heaven came into view when it was finally arranged for her to be taken to the hospital. This was the second and last hospital she would have to enter. Relatively short though her stay at the orphanage had been, she had become very much attached to it and especially to the chapel and the Divine Presence; and of course she had grown very fond of her benefactor. But Mother Godinho assured her she would not abandon her and promised to come to see her every day.

Nevertheless, it was not the same. She was saddened by the absence of the Blessed Sacrament and of the tabernacle she could not see and by the signs of worldliness in the hospital that she could not help but see. We must remember that Our Blessed Lady had introduced her to the mysteries of the life of the spirit when she was still a tender, innocent little child and when she had had practically no contact with the world. As a result, when she did see the world, she saw it almost through the eyes of God. We might say that her first look at temporal things was in the light of eternity. Thus, she could not but immediately and instinctively react unfavorably to all that was not of God or was not in accord with the will of God.

Thus, the dress, the manner and the conversation of visitors in the hospital saddened her, if not by their out-and-out sinfulness, at least by their emptiness of God. "What is it all for?" she would say. "If they only knew what eternity is."

This also explains her attitude toward the doctors. The fact that their thoughts were exclusively for science and medicine, without any consideration of God's part in healing, left her a bit disheartened. "Pity doctors," she said once. "Doctors do not know how to treat their patients with success because they have no love for God."

Perhaps some of us, steeped in worldly wisdom, may be tempted to receive all this with an indulgent smile. But there are other things the little girl said—predictions that came true, for instance—that must give us pause, whether we like it or not, and we cannot deny that these lend weight to all her statements.

A doctor one day requested her prayers for a special intention. "I will pray for you," she assured him, "but just remember that you are going to be taken away, and soon." She told another doctor the same thing about himself and his daughter. Both predictions came true.

Mother Godinho herself one day expressed a great desire to visit the Cova da Iria. Jacinta's quick reply was: "Don't worry, good Mother, you will go there after my death." Which she did.

Another time, before her mother had left the orphanage to return to Aljustrel, Mother Godinho had asked Olimpia if she would not like her two daughters, Florinda and Teresa, to become nuns. "God help me!" the mother had protested.

Jacinta had not heard this conversation. Yet, later she confided to Mother Godinho: "Our Lady would have liked my sisters to become nuns very much. Mother does not want it, and so Our Lady will take them soon to Heaven."

Florinda died of the flu the same year that Jacinta did, and Teresa the next year.

Father De Marchi tells us in *The Crusade of Fatima* that when the doctors first mentioned an operation, Jacinta warned them that it would be useless.

The doctors, however, insisted, but when she was finally taken to the operating room she was found too weak to take gas. Anaesthesia not being then what it is today, the local injection given her by no means took away her pain. Yet she appears to have suffered more from the humiliation of having to expose her body and to place herself in the hands of the strange doctors than from the physical pain.

She was operated on and two ribs were removed. The doctors appeared hopeful of success. But on February 16, she said: "I am not complaining any more. Our Lady has appeared again and said that she is coming for me soon. She took all my pains away." And her doctor testified later that this seems to have been true.

About six o'clock on the evening of February 20, 1920, she said she was not feeling well and asked to receive the Last Rites of the Church. A priest was called, who heard her Confession, but who, trusting to his own judgment, put off Communion until the next morning. But just as Jacinta had warned him, the next morning was too late. For she passed away quietly and alone about 10:30 that same evening.

Doctor Lisboa arranged with a nearby pastor for the casket with her body to be placed in the sacristy of his church. When the news of Jacinta's death got around, however—which it did very quickly—people flocked to see her, and this caused quite a problem for the poor priest. It was finally found necessary to take the coffin to a special room, where only a few visitors at a time were permitted to view her remains. On the 24th, her body was placed in a leaden casket, sealed in the presence of the authorities, and taken to Ourem, accompanied by Mother Godinho. There it was placed in the vault of the Baron of Alvayazere.

Fifteen years later, on September 12, 1935, the Bishop of Leiria commanded that her body be transferred to the cemetery of Fatima, to be placed in the same tomb with the body of Francisco. When Jacinta's casket was opened, her body was found to be still whole and incorrupt. A picture of it was taken, and it was just one more of those privileges I enjoyed that afternoon at Mother Godinho's to be able to see with my own eyes that tiny face, pictured fifteen years after her death, as fresh-looking as that of a sleeping child.

Part III

EPILOGUE
A TRIP TO FATIMA

While I was telling the story of the three children of Fatima on the radio, the desire began to grow within me to go to Portugal and visit some of the places associated with the seers and, if possible, to meet some of the people who knew them who might still be alive. I mentioned this in one of my radio talks, and to my surprise, I received a favorable response from the listeners. Three priests offered to go with me. (All three are now deceased.) I also received letters suggesting friends in Portugal who might be of assistance to me.

Two of these turned out to be very helpful. They were Father Louis Gonzaga de Oliveira, who was in charge of the Beato Nuno Chapel in Lisbon (he was a Carmelite priest) and the other was Mother Mary King, a Sister of St. Dorothy, the first Community Lucia joined after finishing her studies at Vilar. Mother King was Irish and was stationed at a boarding school for girls in a suburb of Porto. Lucia spent her last year or so as a Sister of St. Dorothy in the same convent with Mother King, before leaving to become a cloistered Carmelite in Coimbra. They knew each other well. In fact, they had been in the novitiate together.

Originally, Mother King had been assigned to a house of the Order in London, together with other Irish and British nuns. But during World War II, these sisters had been evacuated to Portugal, whch had not been drawn into the War. This is how it came to pass that Mother King—born in Down Patrick, Ireland—was teaching English at the Colegio do Sardao in Vila Nova de Gaia, when I planned to go to Portugal.

I wrote to her in advance of my trip to inquire if it might be possible to obtain one of the famous hand-carved wooden statues of Our Lady of Fatima sculpted by José Thedim, who made the statue (now in the small chapel or Capelinha in Fatima) that has been venerated by millions of pilgrims. She wrote to say she would get it for me, since she was a personal friend of Thedim.

Our group of four priests left LaGuardia airport on May 9, 1948, arriving in Lisbon on the following day.

We were anxious to say Mass, so we took a cab to the home of Father Louis, who arranged for all four to say Mass in the Carmelite chapel. After our Masses, we invited Father Louis to have lunch with us. He was happy to join us.

After lunch, we rented a car and went sightseeing with Father Louis as our guide. We ended up at the orphanage of Mother Godinho. Father Louis knew her very well. (I have already described this visit, as I told "The Story of Fatima" on the radio.)

When Jacinta had arrived at her orphanage, Mother Godinho related, she gave her a room all by herself on the second floor of the house, with large French windows leading to a tiny balcony overlooking Estrela Park and with a door that connected to the chapel of Our Lady of Miracles next door.

Anxious to tell priests who had come all the way from America about Jacinta, she soon took out and displayed proudly a little blue dress that had been made for Jacinta to wear during the apparitions.

Next, she brought out a brown veil or scarf that the little girl had worn during the apparitions. Only a portion of the scarf is left, and I thought Mother Godinho more than generous when she cut off a piece for each of us priests. Next, she gave each of us a piece of the vest that Francisco had worn during the apparitions. And, to cap it off, she gave each of us a piece of the holmoak tree that Jacinta had brought home to her parents after the unexpected apparition at Valinhos on August 19, 1917.

We took leave of that room with reluctance.

From there we went to the railroad station to purchase tickets for the next day's trip to Vila Nova de Gaia, to meet Mother King. We were able to get seats on the "Espresso" for the long trip north to Porto, where we arrived the next day in the early afternoon. From Porto, we went by cab to the Colegio do Sardao, where Mother King was waiting for us. The Colegio is a boarding school for girls conducted by the Sisters of St. Dorothy.

After supper, we met with the girls during their recreation time, all quite excited to meet priests from America. Later, Mother King informed us that she had already made arrangements for us to stay at the Retreat House at Fatima.

The following day, we left for Fatima by car, with a stop at Coimbra on the way for lunch at another house of the Dorotheans.

We arrived at Fatima about 7:00 p.m. and went directly to the room of Don José Correia da Silva, Bishop of Leiria and Fatima, in the retreat house where all the Bishops of Portugal were finishing their annual retreat. Bishop da Silva spoke no English, but his warm smile was welcome enough for us weary travelers. He had a seminarian take us to the refectory where the Bishops were having their supper. After supper, a few of them gathered around us and welcomed us to Fatima. One of them, when he heard my name was Cirrincione, asked: "Do you speak Italian?" "Some," I replied. "Then, let us talk in Italian," he said. "I studied in Rome and know the language very well" (far better than I did, actually).

He turned out to be Bishop Manuel Maria Ferreira da Silva, Titular Bishop of Gurza. He had taught catechism to Sister Lucia when she was a student at Vilar and had become her confessor and principal spiritual director. Later, he was consecrated a bishop and sent to Goa, India, as Auxiliary to the Archbishop there. Upon his return from India, he was given the task of forming a Portuguese Missionary Society, the post he held at that particular time. Through the years, he was undoubtedly one of the most enthusiastic supporters of the Fatima apparitions among the Portuguese bishops. He was very much impressed by the fact that I was telling the story of Fatima on the radio in America. He seemed intent on providing me with as much material for my talks as possible during my stay.

The next day, Wednesday, May 12, he took us four priests on a whirlwind tour after our Masses, celebrated in the Capelhina, the little chapel built on the spot where the holmoak stood, over which Our Lady had appeared. After breakfast, we rented a car and were soon rolling along the highway to Fatima to visit the church where the three children had been baptized. A short distance from the church was the cemetery where Francisco and Jacinta had been buried. Later, their bodies were exhumed and they now rest on either side of the transept in the Basilica.

From the cemetery, we drove back to Aljustrel and entered Lucia's home, where we met her sister, Maria do Anjos, and her family. It was clear that Bishop Manuel was a frequent visitor there, for he was greeted as an old and beloved friend, everyone coming forward respectfully to kiss his hand. Thence, we proceeded to the home of Francisco and Jacinta, where we received a similar cordial reception from Ti Marto and Ti Olimpia. Ti Marto took us in tow and led us to the well where the three children had been wont to hide from people and where the Angel had appeared once to them. From the well, Ti Marto led the way to Valinhos where Our Lady had appeared on August

19, 1917. Next, he took us to the Cabeco, where the Angel had given Communion to the children. Finally, we returned to Fatima for lunch and a brief break.

That afternoon, we went with the Bishop to welcome back to Fatima the "Pilgrim Virgin" statue, just returning from a tour of Europe and Africa.

By this time, the Cova was filled with thousands of pilgrims, come to celebrate the 13th of May. The observance of the anniversary began at 10:00 p.m. with a candlelight procession, during which the statue of Our Lady was escorted from the Capelinha to a pedestal on the top steps of the Basilica. Bishop Manuel had arranged for me a place near the statue so that I could describe the scene and record the singing by 500,000 voices of the beautiful, plaintive Portuguese hymns in honor of Our Lady. This lasted an hour. It was followed by all-night adoration of the Blessed Sacrament before a monstrance placed to the right, on a small altar.

Wearily, I made my way back to my room about midnight. The Bishop had asked me to accompany him the next morning for the outdoor Mass and blessing of the sick.

But, I never made it. The long overseas flight, the traveling up and down Portugal, the change of climate and food, finally took their toll. When I awakened the next morning, I realized I had the "flu" and a strep throat. I couldn't leave my bed. I thought of the irony of it all. This was the day I had come for. Thousands of native pilgrims had slept on the ground out in the open and were none the worse for it. But I could not leave my bed. Would I ever have another chance?

Our Lady must have smiled as she read my thoughts. For I was to return sixteen more times to Fatima. So much for my trust in the will of God!

Because of the many really sick people who were brought to Fatima on the 13th, there were many doctors there. That afternoon, when the Bishop learned from my friends of my condition, he sent a doctor to my room. He gave me an injection of penicillin. Father De Marchi, on whose book I had relied so much in preparing my radio talks, also came over to visit me.

Was it the penicillin or Divine Providence that had worked a miracle? All I know is that the next morning, I was much improved and planning with Father De Marchi to interview Ti Marto that evening, with my recorder running.

Besides missing the festivities on May 13, there was another disappointment. When I planned to go to Fatima, I had hoped to see Sister Lucia. But when I arrived, I found out that she had entered the Carmelite Monastery in Coimbra just two months before our arrival. She was now a cloistered nun and could have no visitors, outside of members of her family and old friends. I discussed the matter with Bishop Manuel, who agreed that my chances of seeing Sister Lucia were slim.

Our pilgrimage included a trip to Rome. We flew there on Saturday, May 15, taking with us the statue Mother King had obtained for me from

Thedim. I wanted it blessed by the Holy Father, Pope Pius XII. During a semi-private audience with the Holy Father that we were fortunate enough to obtain, he did bless the statue, said a few words to us and gave us his blessing.

I had had the foresight to leave Bishop Manuel the address of the hotel we were going to stay at in Rome. To my surprise and delight, during our week in Rome, I received a letter from the Bishop, suggesting that I obtain a Papal Blessing for Sister Lucia and her Community. "Who knows," he added, "you may be able to present it to her personally."

Naturally, I wasted no time in obtaining the Papal Blessing, looking forward to the possibility of giving it to Sister Lucia. On my return to Portugal from Rome, I met the Bishop at a hotel in Coimbra. I could sense from his manner that things looked good for my meeting with Sister Lucia.

Sure enough, when we arrived at her convent, we were ushered into the visiting room with its formidable iron grating. The whole Community was present, with Reverend Mother Prioress and Sister Lucia in front. I presented the Papal Blessing, leaving it to the Bishop to do the talking, since I do not speak Portuguese. The visit did not last very long, but it lasted long enough for me to realize how blessed by Our Lady I had been throughout this pilgrimage. There could have been only one reason for the signal graces I had received, and that was to continue to spread devotion to the Immaculate Heart of Mary, which was the mission Our Lady had entrusted to Jacinta and which Jacinta had entrusted to Lucia when she bade her goodbye before leaving for the hospital in Lisbon: "Soon I shall go to Heaven. You are to stay here to reveal that Our Lord wants to establish throughout the world the devotion to the Immaculate Heart of Mary. When you reveal this, don't hesitate. Tell everyone that Our Lord grants us all graces through the Immaculate Heart of Mary; that all must make their petitions to her; that the Sacred Heart of Jesus desires that the Immaculate Heart of Mary be venerated at the same time."

Please send details of any favors received through the intercession of Jacinta Marto to the following address: Vice-Postulador da Causa de Jacinta Marto, Apartado 6, P-2496 FATIMA. Codex Portugal.

Moments Divine—Before Bl. Sacrament *Reuter* 10.00
Saints Who Raised/Dead—400 Resurrection Miracles . . 18.50
Wonder of Guadalupe. *Johnston* 9.00
St. Gertrude the Great 2.50
Mystical City of God. (abr.) *Agreda*. 21.00
Abortion: Yes or No? *Grady, M.D.* 3.00
Who Is Padre Pio? *Radio Replies Press* 3.00
What Will Hell Be Like? *St. Alphonsus* 1.50
Life and Glories of St. Joseph. *Thompson* 16.50
Autobiography of St. Margaret Mary 7.50
The Church Teaches. *Documents* 18.00
The Curé D'Ars. *Abbé Francis Trochu* 24.00
What Catholics Believe. *Lovasik* 6.00
Clean Love in Courtship. *Lovasik* 4.50
History of Antichrist. *Huchede*. 4.00
Self-Abandonment to Div. Prov. *de Caussade* 22.50
Canons & Decrees of the Council of Trent 16.50
Love, Peace and Joy. *St. Gertrude/Prévot*. 8.00
St. Joseph Cafasso—Priest of Gallows. *St. J. Bosco* 6.00
Mother of God and Her Glorious Feasts. *O'Laverty* 15.00
Apologetics. *Glenn* 12.50
Isabella of Spain. *William Thomas Walsh* 24.00
Philip II. P.B. *William Thomas Walsh* 37.50
Fundamentals of Catholic Dogma. *Ott* 27.50
Creation Rediscovered. *Keane* 21.00
Hidden Treasure—Holy Mass. *St. Leonard* 7.50
St. Philomena. *Mohr* 12.00
St. Philip Neri. *Matthews*. 7.50
Martyrs of the Coliseum. *O'Reilly* 21.00
Thirty Favorite Novenas 1.50
Devotion to Infant Jesus of Prague 1.50
On Freemasonry *(Humanum Genus). Leo XIII* 2.50
Thoughts of the Curé D'Ars. *St. John Vianney* 3.00
Way of the Cross. *St. Alphonsus Liguori* 1.50
Way of the Cross. *Franciscan* 1.50
Magnificent Prayers. *St. Bridget of Sweden* 2.00
Conversation with Christ. *Rohrbach* 12.50
Douay-Rheims New Testament. 16.50
Life of Christ. 4 vols. P.B. *Emmerich*. (Reg. 75.00) 60.00
The Ways of Mental Prayer. *Lehodey* 16.50

Prices subject to change.